Steve Legg & Jude Simpson

31 Bedtime Prayers and Poems For Kids

Copyright © Steve Legg & Jude Simpson

First published in 2024 by SCM
(Son Christian Media Ltd.)

The right of Steve Legg & Jude Simpson to be identified as the authors of this work has been asserted by them in accordance with the Copyright, Designs and Patents Act 1988. All rights reserved.

No part of this publication may be reproduced, stored in a retrieval system, or transmitted in any other form or by any means, electronic, mechanical, photocopying, recording, or otherwise, without the prior permission of the publisher, except in the case of brief quotations embodied in critical articles or reviews.

British Library Cataloguing in Publication Data.
A catalogue record for this book is available from the British Library.

Cover design, typesetting and Illustration by
Andy S. Gray, Onegraydot Ltd.
onegraydot.com | LinkedIn Onegraydot

Typeset in Gill Sans Nova

Special Thanks

For A,L,B and J,
who inspired many of
the lines in this book!

Contents

Left Angle
Wrap Me In Peace
Juggling Chickens
What a Day!
Goodnight Sun
Conversation with God
Heavenly Sounds
Drop, Drip, Sleep, Slip
When the Nattering Stops
That Day is Done
A Prayer for days when I feel like being Silly
In Your Presence
When somebody is mean
Yumminess
Delete as Applicable prayer
Help me to pray
I've heard of your Light
As Elephants Love Waterholes
Guardian Angel
Please God
Cheerleader, Bodyguard

God and my Teddy

The Best Rest (a bedtime tongue-twister)

Whatever we Have, Whatever we Lack

Unconditional

You Know

Knitting

Friends and Family

A Prayer for Difficult Days

Your Love is Enough

Climbing the Mountain of Sleep

To
Marla

Steve Legg & Jude Simpson
31 Bedtime Prayers AND Poems For Kids

Bedtime!

Does that word fill you with dread at the idea of trying to wrestle your fidgety little octopus into bed again, or do you cherish the thought of settling down sleepily and sharing the last, precious minutes of the day together?

If you're anything like us, bedtime with little ones can feel like an unpredictable mixture of treasured moments and infuriating disarray! Yet it's a crucial time of connection, that we long to make the most of.

We have created this collection of bedtime poems and prayers to cater for all kinds of moods and moments. Some are heartfelt and lyrical, some are funny or silly. Some express repentance, or offer God our sadness, while others give thanks for the good things in life, or look forward to the next day of curiousity and adventure.

Above all, these prayers and poems have been designed to communicate deep truths about God and ourselves, in ways that are accessible and memorable for young children.

Picture this: cosy pyjamas, snuggly blankets, and a copy of this book in hand. As you flip through the pages, you'll discover a treasure trove of rhymes, rhythms, and prayers designed to spark imagination, inspire gratitude, and send little ones off to dreamland with hearts full of faith, hope, and joy.

So, grab their favourite teddy, dim the lights, and let the bedtime adventure begin!

Steve Legg   and   Jude Simpson

Left Angle

Is there such a thing as a left angle?
Can you teach knitting to sheep?
Tomorrow, I'll keep being curious,
But now I am going to sleep.

Can you make music from tuna?
Do boars ever get bored?
Tomorrow, I'll let my mind wander,
Now, bed's what I'm going towards.

Why can't computers play tennis?
Do Kangaroos ever cough?
Tomorrow, I'll search for the answers,
But now, Lord, please help me switch off!

Wrap me in peace

Lord, as I close my eyes to sleep,
Wrap me in peace, so warm and deep.

Roll me in relaxation and calm,
Hold me in hope, like caring arms.

Cloak me in confidence, strong and true,
Help me be me, surrounded by you.

What a day!

What a day! What a day!
    Lots of work and lots of play!
        Lots to eat and lots to drink!
            Lots to say and lots to think!

What a day! What a day!
    Lots to hear and lots to say!
        Lots to do - so much to fit!
            Thank you, God, for all of it.

Goodnight Sun

Goodnight Sun,
Have a good night.
Hello Stars,
Twinkling bright.

                                        Welcome Moon,
                                        Glistening sphere.
                                            You up there
                                      And me down here.

God made Sun,
Shining and warm.
God made Stars,
Travelling forms.

                                        God made Moon,
                                        Silver like shell.
                                            He made you
                                      And me as well.

Drop, Drip, Sleep, Slip

I'm just a drop in the ocean.

I'm just a drop drip drop in the ocean.

I'm just a drop drip drop drip drop in the ocean.

But in that sea, God sees me.

I'm just a sleeping slip of a child.

I'm just a sleeping slip sleep slip of a child.

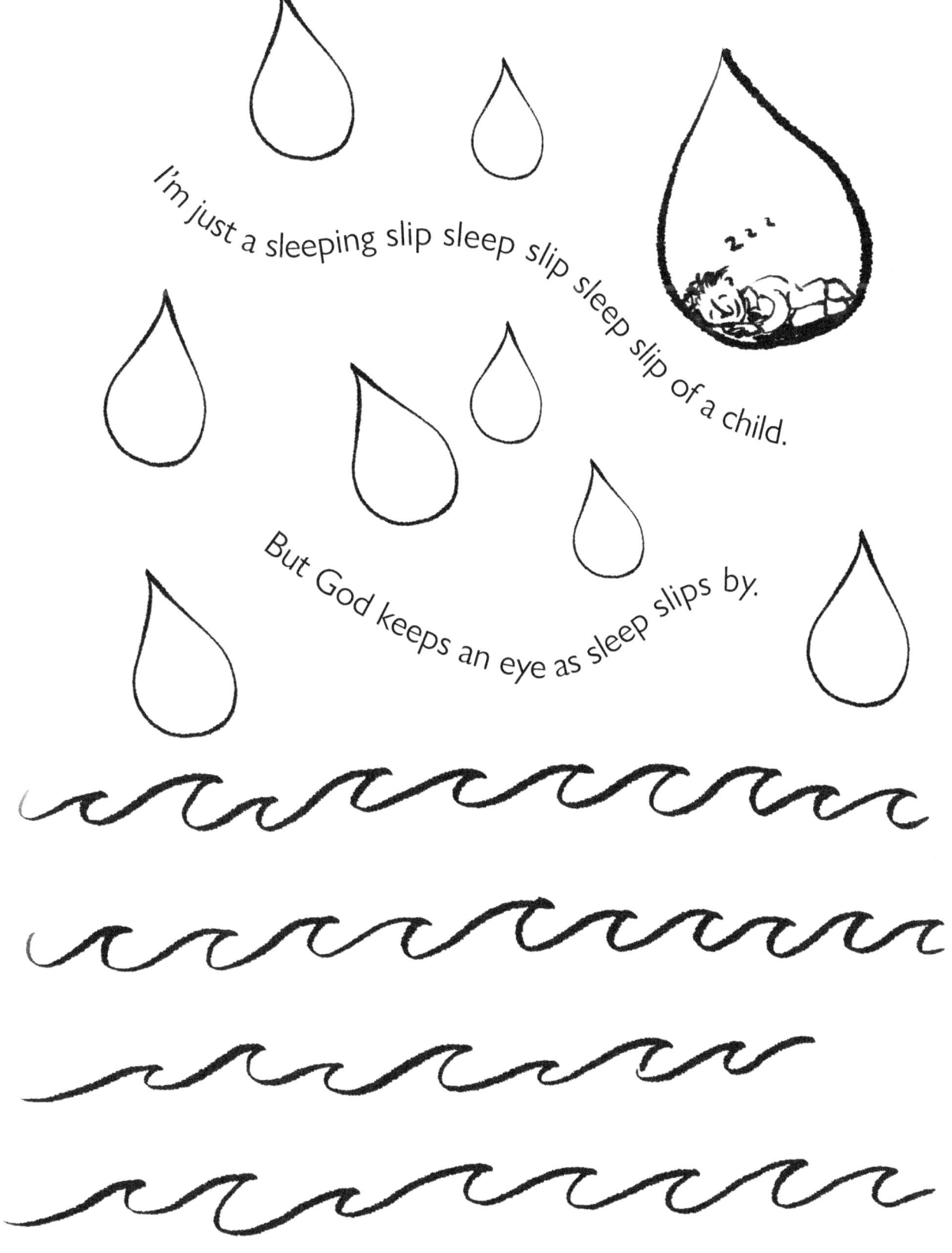

Heavenly Sounds

You are the creaky crunch of snow
under winter boots.

You are the soft and silent swing
of a falling leaf.

You are the ping of a new message
from a best friend.

You are the hug of silence
when someone stops drilling.

You are the sigh of relief
when a lost thing is found.

Lullaby, Lord, fill my nighttime
with heavenly sounds.

That Day is Done

Dear God,
Well, there you go, that day is done.
Thanking you is Number One –
Thank you for the smiles and fun.

Here are three things I am thankful for today:
1.
2.
3.

Well, there you go, that day is through.
Saying Sorry's Number Two –
I apologise to you:

Here are between 1 and 33 things I apologise and ask forgiveness for today:
1.
2.
3.

Well, there goes that day, as you see.
Asking you is Number Three —
Some for others, some for me.

Here are three requests I'd like to make today,
either for myself or for others:
1.
2.
3.

That day's done, there will be more.
Praising you is Number Four.
All the blessings which you pour.

Here are three things about you that I praise you
for today:
1.
2.
3.

Well, there you go, that day is done.
Tomorrow is another one
Not yet begun.
How exciting!!

When the nattering stops…

When the nattering stops and the chattering's done…
When the dinging and pinging are quiet and gone…
When there's no noise annoying me, just a faint hum...
Like the background to sleepiness, Jesus, please come.

Come with your song, so soothing and deep.
Come with your breathing that steadies my sleep.
Come with your whisper; that's sweet like a rhyme.
Come with your heart that beats next to mine.

A prayer for days when I feel like being Silly.

Thank you, God, that I didn't turn into a ginger cake today.

Thank you, God, that I didn't wake up with daffodils growing out of my nose today.

Thank you, God, that nobody told me I had to change my name to
"Pock-Weffle Compy-Noo" today.

Thank you for all the things I sometimes
take for granted
and thank you for silliness.

Amen*

*If any of these things happen to you today, please get in touch, and we will give you your money back!

In Your Presence

(inspired by Psalm 27)

Dear God, what I'd really love —
what I'd really, really love —
Is to rest in a room where you are;
Stand on a tower with you,
looking out at the world;
Learn from you what it's like
to be totally good;
Curl up on your window seat,
reading your book;
Hang out with you and
watch you chat with people;
Lie on my back, looking up at the sky and
thinking about you
All my life long.

Yumminess

You are the milkslurp at breakfast,
The zing-zip of time for packed lunch.
You made everything delicious.
You are a pink–apple–crunch.

You are the smell of bread baking,
The fragrance of purple sweet pea.
You are the breathe-deep of yumminess
When Dad's cooked my favourite tea.

When somebody is mean

When somebody is mean to me
    I feel like you've forgotten me.
        I feel, in my mind,
    That I might break like pottery.
        Help me to remind myself
        That you are always kind,
Unshiftable as mountains—
    The best friend I could find.

When somebody is mean to me
    I feel my heart is breaking.
        I feel frustrated, small and weak,
        The ground beneath me shaking.
        But you are stronger than they are—
        I will not be destroyed.
I'll lean on you—unchanging rock—
    And be filled with your joy.

(Delete as Applicable) prayer

Dear God,

Let me tell you about today. It was …
completely amazing / totally rubbish / surprisingly unusual / majorly exciting / slightly disappointing / frankly normal / same as ever / beyond my wildest dreams—even the dreams about astronauts with robot parrots.

I'm sorry about the …
mean thing I said / bad thing I did / person I didn't listen to / instruction I should have followed / incident with the custard and the tea towel …

Thank you for your forgiveness and love, and thank you for…
my brothers and sisters / art lessons / football / good teachers / fun times with friends / music / beautiful singing / enthusiastic singing / terrible singing that still made us laugh / playtimes / the sound of birds singing / snow / space / huge lumps of blu-tac.

When I think of tomorrow, I'm feeling …
pretty excited / seriously scared /
warm and fuzzy / slightly nervous / utterly thrilled /
as bored as a woodpecker in a sandpit.

Thank you, that whatever happened today and
whatever might happen tomorrow,
You are always applicable
And you can't be deleted.

Amen.

(If nothing in the list is applicable,
you could make up your own)

Help me to pray

Help me to pray and not to worry.

Help me to pray and not to blame.

Help me to pray in faith, trusting.

Help me to pray, in Jesus' name.

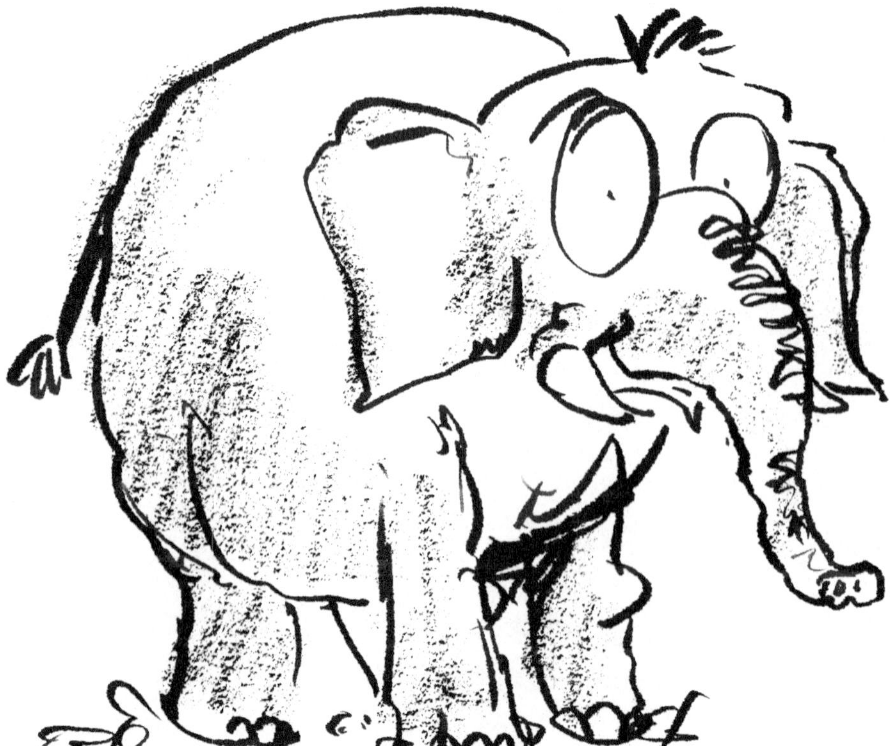

As Elephants love Waterholes
(inspired by Psalm 42)

I really long to know you, Lord,
As elephants love waterholes.

I'm thirsty for your friendship, Lord,
Like river-dwelling water voles.

I want to build my life round you,
Like beavers build their homes,

To do your work and know your ways,
Like bees in honeycomb.

I've heard of your Light

I've heard of your Light
—a candle in the darkness.
I've heard of your Light
—sunrays through the clouds.
I've heard of your Light
—a face that shines with laughter.
I've heard of your Light
—phone screens in a crowd.

I've heard of your Light
—fireworks in the Autumn.
I've heard of your Light
—dazzling sandy shores.
I've heard of your Light
—the glimmer of a sunrise.

I'm turning off my Light,
but you never turn off yours.

Please God

       Please, God, could I have…

Sleep that's as sweet as a warm apple pie,

       Rest warm and long like the sun in July,

Peace like a stream that keeps rippling by,

       Waking that's clear as a blue-puddle sky.

Guardian Angel

Could you put an angel
    at the end of my bed?
Halo bright and shiny,
    golden wings outspread.
I'll tuck all my worries
    into his back pocket,
My fears in a box
    so he can shut and lock it.
He'll look out for danger,
    protect me while I sleep
Safely in God's castle—
    peaceful, long and deep.

His feather wings will shield me.
    I won't have any fear—
I'll know I'm in your presence when
    I feel him standing near.
He'll send away my enemies—
    bad dreams and scary thoughts,
His shadow like a shelter—
    his arms like towering forts.
He'll always go where I go—
    although he can't be seen.
I'll always sleep nearby him—
    assured, calm, and serene.

Cheerleader, Bodyguard

You are my armour and my bodyguard
    So I don't need to be afraid.
You are my instructor and my cheerleader
    So I don't need to worry.
Even though children are spiteful to me
    You're never spiteful.
Even when teachers are harsh with me
    You're never harsh with me.
Even when someone I thought was my best friend
                        laughs at me
    You never laugh at me.

So whatever happens, I'll hold my head high
Because I am your child,

And you are my king, my keyworker, my tutor, my
Parent, my carer and my best friend,
All rolled into one.

Wow!

God and My Teddy

There are just a few small differences
Between my teddy and God—
> **One's a heavenly being,**
> *One looks a little bit odd.*
> **One doesn't have a body,**
> *The other lost one of his ears.*
> **One gives my heart peace and comfort,**
> *One can soak up my tears.*

There are some important differences
Between God and my Teddy—
> *One's losing some of his stuffing,*
> **One's powerful and rock-steady.**
> *One can fit under my armpit,*
> **One set the planets to spin.**
> *One once got stuck down the sofa,*
> **One freed the whole world from sin.**

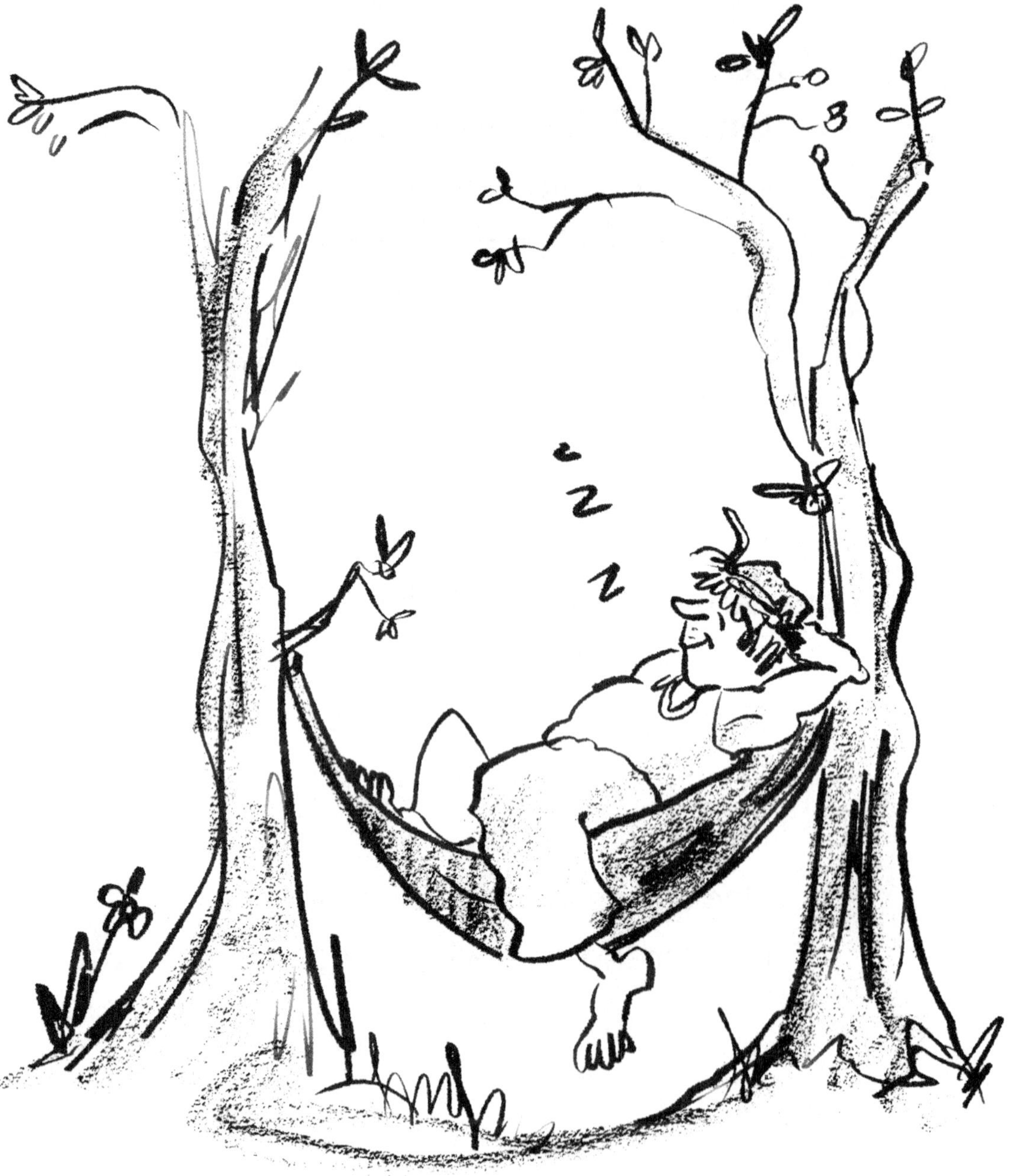

Conversation with God

Do you snore? Do you snuffle?
Do you roll up in the sheets?
Do you dream? Do you dribble?
        "No, no – I never sleep!"

Do you sleepwalk? Do you fidget?
Do your earlobes sometimes shake?
Does your leg hang out the side?
        "No, I just stay wide awake!"

Do your eyelids flick and flutter?
Do you ever bang your head?
Does your mouth hang open wide?
        "No – I never go to bed!"

If you never go to bed at all,
then what is it you do?
        "I stay up all night long,
          watching over you."

The Best Rest
(a bedtime tongue-twister)

> The best rest is blessed rest—
> The rest is less successful rest.

(How many times running can you say it through?
How fast can you go?)

Whatever we Have, Whatever we Lack

As the evening starts to end,
Thank you for this day:
>   Thank you for food that fed me.
>   Thank you for clothes that protected me.
>   Thank you for education, equipping me.
>   Thank you for grown-ups who guided me.
>   Thank you for home, where I'm nurtured.

Thank you for the love that
makes my life meaningful,
Whatever I have and whatever I may lack.

As the morning dawns tomorrow,
I'll think of other children:
>   Feed those who are hungry, Lord.
>   Clothe those who need protection, Lord.
>   Teach those who need education, Lord.
>   Lead grown-ups to those who need
>   guidance, Lord.
>   Find homes for those who need them, Lord.

Thanks for your love that flows to us all,
Whatever we have and whatever we may lack.

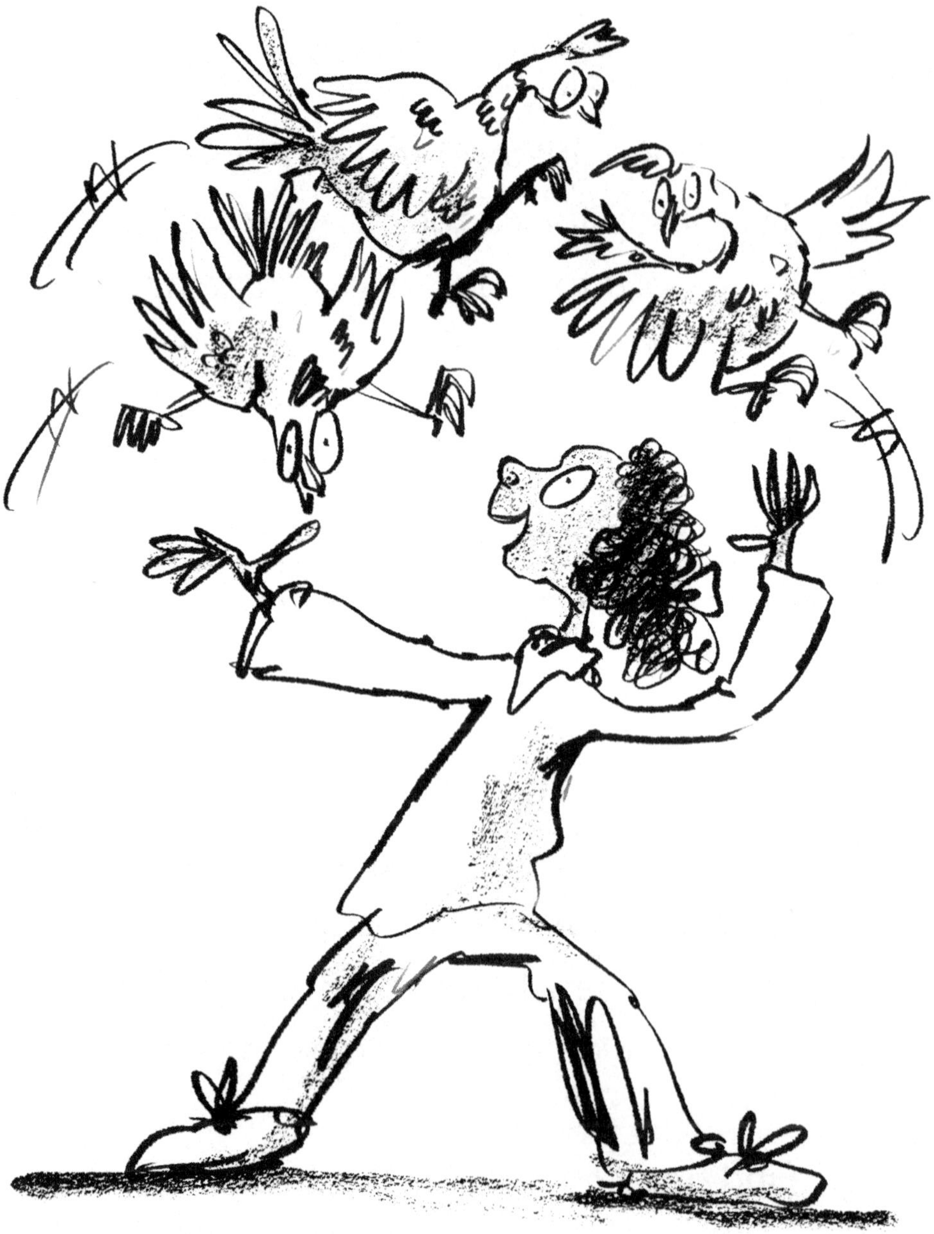

Juggling chickens

I could walk a thousand miles,
Jump higher than a crane,
and although you'd be impressed,
you'd love me just the same.

I could juggle twenty chickens
And forty-seven geese,
But although you'd be surprised,
Your love would not increase.

I could earn the most points ever
And beat my highest score,
But although you'd think that pretty cool,
You'd still not love me more.

I don't need to deserve you,
Impress you or be clever.
Your love could not be bigger -
It's already the biggest ever.

Unconditional

Dear God,
Guess what.
I need your forgiveness
AGAIN!

I'm sorry, God, for what I did.
It wasn't right, and it wasn't good.
I'm going to try not to do it any more.
I'm going to try and do good stuff instead.

Thank you, God,
That your forgiveness comes
Every time we need it
Even when that means
        Every
                Single
                        Day.

Wow! Your love really is
        Unconditional.
Amen

Knitting
(inspired by Psalm 139)

They say you were there,
    right at the start of me—
Knitted together my bones,
    veins and arteries.
You wove your love right
    into the heart of me.
Yes, every part of me,
You made it, God.

Was it like crochet or more like
    construction?
Did you just wing it or use some
    instructions?
Did you need screwdrivers?
    Did you use suction?
Yes, every part of me,
You made it, God.

                    In a room full of duvets,
              you know which one's mine—
                    You know the colour,
                  you know the design.
            Even when changing and growing,
                        you still know
            The shape of the dent my head makes
                            on my pillow.

You sculpted this body—
    the one I was born in—
The eyelids now drooping,
    the lips that are yawning
I'll rest now with confidence
    and see you in the morning—
Yes, every part of me,
You made it, God.

You know
(inspired by Psalm 139)

All my secrets, all my dreams,
My silent thoughts, my rowdy screams,
My kindest wish, my nastiest whim,
My happy mood, when I feel grim,
The ins and outs, the ups, the downs,
The consequences and the crowns,
The stand-up tall, the tired flop,
You know it all, bottom to top.

You know my head, my feet, my toes,
My freckles, creases, ears and lobes,
My outside skin, the inside me—
You'd even recognise my knees!
You see me stand or sit instead,
And now, when I lie down in bed,
You see me sleep, and this is clear—
when I wake up, you'll still be here.

Friends and family

Bless my friends and family,
Bless my dad and mum,
Bless my brothers, sisters,
Every single one.

Bless my great-grandparents,
(and my grandparents—they're great!)
Cousins, siblings, parents, carers,
Chums and friends and mates.

Bless my half- and step-siblings,
The big ones and the small,
My step-parents and godparents—
Surely that's them all?!

Nieces, nephews, aunts and uncles,
Wow, there are a lot—
My foster–relatives as well.
Is there anyone I forgot?

Lord, bless those who love me,
Wherever they may be.
Oh yes—there's one thing I forgot.
Dear God, please bless me!

A prayer for difficult days

Tonight, my heart feels sad and heavy,
It's not that surprising—
The world is full of yucky stuff,
And things that stop me smiling.
I'll shut my eyes and think of you—
You give me what I need.
You are my heavenly parent,
Your love is guaranteed.

You didn't leave us in this mess,
You came and got involved.
You gave yourself so we could live—
And see our pain resolved.
You sunk right in then burst back up,
You took our gunk with you.
However ick the world may feel,
I know your light shines through.

Your love is enough

There are a few things I would really like:
Books about dragons, a brand-new bike,
A cinema trip, some cool stuff to wear
    (or stick on my nails)…(or put in my hair)
Lots more computer games, cuddly toys,
Glitter balls that make a glittery noise.
Magical unicorns, enchanted swords,
    Tiny cute animal figures to horde.
Plastic play kitchens and workbench tools,
Table football, air hockey and pool.
Help me remember, although these are fun,
There's only one thing I need—yes, only one.

Nothing's essential compared to your love,
Even if I had nothing, your love is enough.

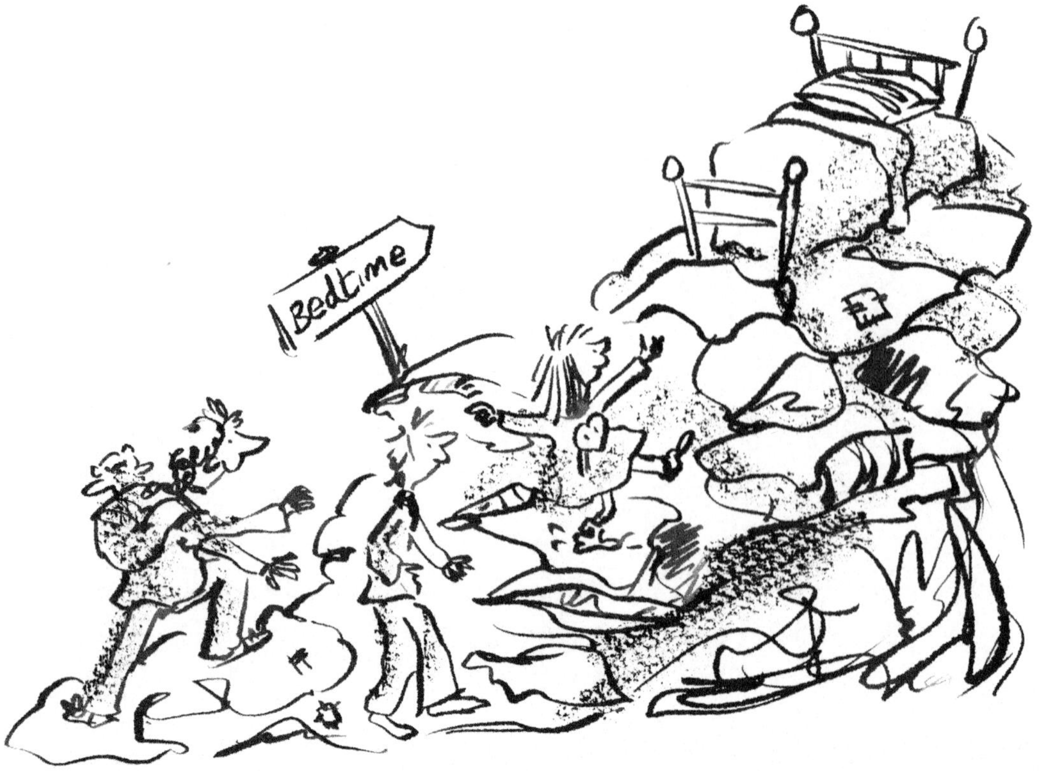
Bedtime

Climbing the Mountain of Sleep

I'm climbing the mountain of sleep
It's steep! It's steep!

I'll wade in the meadow of dreams
Through streams! Through streams!

I'm walking the pathway to rest
A quest! A quest!

I've opened the door to shuteye

    Goodbye!

        (yawn!)

            Goodbye!

                (yawn!)

                    Goodbye!

About the authors

Jude Simpson is a poet, lyricist, author and performer. She writes for adults and children, and her work is known for its witty wordplay, quirky humour and sheer joyfulness.
A veteran of Edinburgh, Glastonbury and Greenbelt, Jude is a regular on Konnect Radio and at Big Church Festival. She performs at poetry clubs, festivals, churches and theatres nationwide. She writes school musicals for The Little Musicals Company, and her children's show "A Noise Annoys" is currently in development at the Junction Theatre, Cambridge.
Jude also hosts literature events and co-authors biographies and memoirs. Find out more at judesimpson.co.uk

Steve's infectious blend of humour, magic, and evangelism has captivated audiences across the globe since 1988. As an international entertainer and speaker, he has left audiences both baffled and inspired. He has worked in over 25 countries and performed at the NIA Birmingham, Wembley Conference Centre and The Royal Albert Hall, to name just three. Beyond the stage, Steve is the visionary behind Sorted, the world's most wholesome men's magazine, and is an award-winning author with 18 books under his belt. He and his wife, Bekah, live in the coastal town of Littlehampton and have five grown-up daughters, one granddaughter, a shed, and a dog, Colbie.

OTHER BOOKS BY STEVE LEGG

Making Friends - Evangelism the easy way
Man, Myth, or Maybe More
Big Questions
The A-Z of Evangelism
Firm Foundations
The A-Z of Christmas
The Chancer
Paper Thongs and Further Misadventures
The Last Laugh
The Last Laugh Journal

BOOKS STEVE WROTE WITH ALEXA TEWKESBURY

It's a Boy!
Lions, Whales, and Thrilling Tales
The Lying Tree
CyberSky

BOOKS STEVE WROTE WITH BEKAH LEGG

All Together
Life Together
Time Together
Growing Together
Advent Together

OTHER BOOKS BY JUDE SIMPSON

Shambolic Mammal – poems, lyrics, wordplay and musings

How Big could a thank you be?

BOOKS JUDE WROTE WITH KEVIN DUNCAN

Friends, Foes and Fossils – the Mary Anning Musical

BOOKS JUDE WROTE WITH VAL JEAL

Broken By Love – Transforming the lives of women on the streets of Bristol

BOOKS JUDE WROTE WITH e:merge

Just Walk With Me – a true story of inner city youth work

About the illustrator

Andy S. Gray is illustrator of the award winning *Whistlestop Tales*, and many other titles over the last 20 years. He's a Church of England minister, visual consultant, and graphic recorder. He's worked professionally with children and young people for over 30 years in schools and churches. He is proud to be autistic, and encourages people to embrace their uniqueness and live life to the full.

You can see more of his work on most social media by searching @onegraydot, and at onegraydot.com

Printed in Great Britain
by Amazon